1
TOM'S SECRET

"Hey there, Jack!" Jack Field turned and saw his friend Tom running towards him. "Coming over the lines with me?" The newly laid railway lines were like a magnet to Jack. Always drawing him there. He grinned, dropped his hedging knife, and kicked it under the hedge.

"Race you then."

The two boys sped over the field and up the bank to where the silver lines gleamed below them in the September sunshine. Jack could hardly believe the new Liverpool to Manchester Railway would be passing through their village. Tom began whistling cockily.

"I've got a secret, a secret."

"Tell me then."

"A secret, a se-ee-cret," went on Tom.

"Don't believe you."

"I have, and it's steaming hot, STEAMING!" Jack grabbed Tom's wrist.

"TELL ME for goodness sake!" Tom laughed.

"The Stephensons' steam locomotive has arrived in Liverpool." Jack's eyes opened wide.

"What, 'Rocket'?"

"*Yes*, all the way from Robert Stephenson's engineering works in Newcastle. It came down the canals." Jack nudged his friend on the arm.

"Just half a day's walk away man. Let's go and see it?"

"No need. Uncle Will says it will be up here in no time, practising for the engine trials." A rush of excitement flooded through Jack. Trials had been organised to find the best engine to pull trains on this new railway line. There was a prize of £500 for the winner of the competition, and the whole world seemed to have gone crazy thinking up daft ideas. But the Stephensons' engine was special. Designed by George Stephenson and built by his son Robert, it wasn't a horse-drawn engine, but an iron animal with fire in its belly.

"I bet it flames like a Christmas pudding."

"Silly ass!" Tom gave him a push and Jack fell and went rolling back down the hillside. He got up laughing.

Then he stopped laughing. At the far end of the field a man was pushing sheep back through a gap in the hedge – the gap he, Jack, should have mended. It was his father and he was in a fury.

"YOU WRETCHED SON OF MINE. You and that cursed railway. It's not the railway that provides your bread, Jack. It's farming this land. Do you hear?" Jack sighed.

"Yes, Father. I hear."

2
IN THE RAILWAY TAVERN

Jack knew the only way to win back his father's favour was to work hard. The next day he was up before dawn, feeding the cows and then into the barn, threshing wheat hour after hour.

That evening as the sun disappeared beneath rosy clouds he saw Tom's dark silhouette beckoning from the farm gate.

"You should see
our inn. It's all trimmed
up with flags ready for
the trials and Ma's
changed the name
from 'Coaching Inn' to
'The Railway Tavern'.
My Uncle Will's
supping ale there.
Coming over, Jack?"

"I am!" The tiredness that had been
with Jack since midday fell away. Tom's
Uncle Will was great. He was one of the
chief railway engineers on the new line.

When Jack entered the inn, the first
person he saw was Will Allcard sitting by
the fire. He was finding it hard to read
the *Liverpool Mercury* with the inn's
green parrot zooming round the room.
It landed on his head and squawked. Will
laughed loudly and nodded to Jack.

"Robert Stephenson kept parrots, you know – when he was in South America searching for minerals, four years gone. Had monkeys too. Loves animals he does." Will shook his head and the bird flew off. "You've heard about 'Rocket' arriving then, Jack?" Jack nodded. "Brilliant men, the Stephensons, particularly Robert," went on Will, "he's building bridges too and working on the Canterbury and Whitstable railway line."

Will chuckled, "Not bad for a fellow who's just got wed, eh?" He folded up his newspaper. "You will be coming to the trials won't you, Jack? It's history in the making, lad. *Nothing* like this has ever happened before."

"Of course he will," answered Tom. "Everyone will."

3
A COUPLE OF CHIMNEYS

"Time off for the trials, Jack. What next?"
his father was eating breakfast, his bad
leg resting on a stool. "There's all that
wheat to thresh and get to the corn
merchant."

"But Father…"

"…Those Stephenson fellers should stick to making engines for coal mines. We don't want engines thundering by, setting fire to the land, and scattering sheep. And as for that bloomin' great viaduct, stuck up like a fistful of fingers down Sankey Brook."

Jack turned away. He couldn't bear to listen. He'd seen the navvies building Robert Stephenson's viaduct, watched the pillars of stone rise above the canal. He could just imagine the excitement of seeing an engine steam across. Taking a hunk of bread from the table Jack went out into the damp morning.

By midday his arms ached like they had lead weights for muscles. He threw the threshing stick into the corner of the barn and went to get Lady the horse. Then he rode her out across the fields against the fresh morning breeze.

Halfway down the hillside he pulled Lady to a standstill. A group of men were coming along the turnpike road below. They were pulling a cart, and on the cart was something with a tall chimney.

Suddenly a black
top hat came twirling
over the hedge and
bowled past him.
Jack rode after it, then lowering
himself to the ground, reached for it. But
the topper twisted neatly out of his way.
Jack chased it. Then lunging forward he
grabbed the hat and ran down to the
roadside with it.

The men cheered and a tall smiling man with thick wavy hair stepped forward. Jack handed him the top hat and everyone clapped.

"Nearly lost my chimney stack that time!" said the man. He set the top hat firmly on his head. "I'm most obliged, lad. Thanks!"

But Jack wasn't listening. He was
looking at the tall grey chimney
belonging to the yellow
engine up on the cart.
He saw the brass plaque
twinkling on its side.

He could recognise the letter R and O,
and the letter T at the end. The man
slapped the side of the engine. "What do
you think of her then? Come and watch
us unload her." Jack's spirits soared but
then quickly sank as he remembered
the wheat.

"I… I can't. I've got work to do, Sir, Mister… er…"

"Stephenson," said the man, "Robert Stephenson." He reached out and shook Jack's hand warmly. "Well, you must come to the trials and see 'Rocket' perform then."

"I will, Sir. I will." He watched the engine go down the road. No one was going to stop him, no one.

4

SEE YOU AT THE TRIALS

Jack burst into the scullery where Tom was churning butter. "Guess who I've just seen."

"A ghost!"

"No stupid, the great man himself."

"Oh, you mean your father!"

"*No no no!* Robert Stephenson no less!" Tom laughed in disbelief.

"Seen him, seen him…" Jack dipped
his hand into the butter. He chased Tom
out of the scullery but skidded slap into
Tom's mother in the doorway.

"Jack Field, I'll skin
you alive," she said and
Tom pulled a stupid face
at him and laughed.

"Sorry, Mrs Green, but Mr Stephenson asked me what I thought of 'Rocket'. Shook this hand he did."
He held up the other hand.
"And this hand touched 'Rocket'."
They all burst out laughing.

Then, with the words tumbling out of his mouth with excitement Jack told the story of the hat.

The next few days Jack worked like he'd never worked before. He finished the threshing the day before the trials and found Tom walking along the lines, looking at the new stand there.

"The grain's all in sacks and on the cart, Tom. We've only got to take it down to Joe Archer's place this afternoon. I'll be able to see the trials." Tom thrust his fist into the air.

"Great! Get over early in the morning. We'll see everything brilliantly from my bedroom window. Uncle Will's got us a printed programme."

"Must go," said Jack. "See you tomorrow."

"Remember *real* early mate."

"First light," promised Jack.

But when Jack got home ready to take the wheat his father was hobbling round the room and throwing his hands up in despair.

"Joe Archer's barn's gone up in flames," he said. "Everything burned to the ground. He'll not take our wheat, Jack. We'll have to look for someone to buy it tomorrow."

5
LONG JOURNEY

Jack thumped down in the chair, all the strength draining out of him. He couldn't believe it.

"Your father's right, Jack," said his mother. "We really need the money." She poured him a mug of weak tea. Jack swilled back the tea and stood up.

"I'm going out," he said flatly.

Tom was horrified
when he heard the news.

"You can't miss the
first day, Jack…
You just can't.
Everybody will
be there!"

"Not me," said
Jack glumly.

"Take the wheat somewhere else."

"Oh *yes*, where?" His friend shrugged.

"Well I know of nowhere…"

"…Tom!" Jack interrupted. "Tom, I've just thought. There's Liverpool! What do you say? Let's go right now and find a buyer." He saw the smile creep onto Tom's face. Then Tom was grabbing his cap off the table and shoving him out of the doorway.

"Get going man before I'm missed."

Jack harnessed Lady to the cart and they were down by 'The Ship Inn' before the four o'clock stage coach left Rainhill. Mr Bartholomew, sitting on the wall there, whilst his four horses drank from the trough, waved to them.

"Ten miles an hour, old Barty says his Liverpool Umpire goes," said Tom. "'Rocket' will beat that I bet." He moved nearer Jack and Jack pulled up his shirt collar. There was a coldness in the air and the light was already fading. It would be a long journey.

Lady trotted along the cobbled road
past the milestones until Liverpool
reached out to them with its big
buildings and crowds of people.

"They're all here for the engine trials,"
said Tom. "Look there's a notice over
there on that lamp post. I bet every
lodging house in Liverpool is full." But
Jack wasn't listening. He was looking for
corn merchants.

"We'd best go down by the docks," he
said, jumping off the cart.

Through the streets of gaslight and
shadows they went. On and on until the
streets got narrower and filthier and
Jack felt his stomach tighten with fear.
Then still further and he began to wish
they'd never come. A man, slumped
against a lamp post, stared at them with
glassy eyes.

"Ask him where there's a corn place," said Tom. The man leered at them and held out his hand.

"Have you any money then?" he said. Jack shook his head.

"You can have this," said Tom taking a slab of cake from his pocket. The man pounced on it hungrily.

"There's Jimmy Holt's place round the next corner, near the Crown Tunnel."

It wasn't far but just as they arrived a man was dragging the big barn gate shut.

"Hey mister, mister," yelled Jack. "We've got wheat."

"Come back with it tomorrow," the man called.

"Can't." The man moaned but opened the gate. "You'll have to unload it yourselves."

Much later, they left his office, tired
and hungry but with the money safely
inside their shirts. Jack glanced at the
entrance to the Crown Tunnel as they
passed by. George Stephenson, Robert's
father had recently finished building it.

"You can go through for a shilling,"
Tom said. "They say it's huge. It's painted
white inside and lit up." But Jack was
suddenly starving hungry. He gave a
gentle tug on the reins.

"Home, Lady. Home, girl."

His mother leapt to her feet as he opened the parlour door. "Jack…! Where *on earth* have you been?" Jack took out the heavy bags of money from his shirt and handed them to his father.

"Liverpool. I sold every grain of wheat, Father. And I got the best grain prices."

6
THE ROAR OF STEAM

The flags were flying. The band was
playing as Jack squeezed happily
through the hoards of people, and made
his way towards 'The Railway Tavern'.

He went up the stairs and opened the
bedroom door to find Tom leaning out
of the window.

"Quick, Jack. 'Rocket's' pulling a train-load of directors. They're all wearing white ribbons." Jack rushed forwards to look. A jet of steam that had leapt from the yellow engine, frightening the crowds, came drifting up towards them. Jack stuck his face out of the window.

"Oh smell it, Tom. It smells of speed!"

"You're daft as a dormouse, Jack Field, you are."

"And I can see its fire," shrieked Jack. Tom pulled him back from the window and began pointing out the various engines.

"That one with the red wheels is called 'Perseverance'. It fell off the cart on its way here and is being mended. And the blue one is 'Novelty'."

"What about the one with the caged horse?" said Jack. "It looks like something from a fair. And whatever is that thing?" Two men were winding an engine along the tracks, and the crowds hanging over the Rainhill bridge were laughing and cheering at them. "Oh let's go outside Tom·with everyone else."

They found Uncle Will talking to his friend Jack Raistrick, who was one of the judges.

"*Nothing* but a showpiece that 'Novelty'," Will was saying.

"But twenty-eight miles an hour, Will," they heard the judge reply, "and definitely the favourite so far."

The band started up again and drowned the conversation. 'Rocket' was steaming, ready to go once more.

All through the day 'Rocket' tirelessly zoomed up and down. All day they watched her.

"She'll win," said Uncle Will. "Mark my words. Tough as a battleship she is. By the end of the week the other engines will be in bits."

Five days later their excitement knew no bounds for 'Novelty's' boiler gave way, knocking the engine out of the competition.

The green and yellow engine called 'Sans Pareil' had burned out its pump the day before, leaving 'Perseverance' which was chugging along at only six miles an hour. Uncle Will laughed as that too withdrew from the competition.

Meanwhile 'Rocket' carried on cheekily up and down the line, between the marked posts. As it puffed to a halt Uncle Will put his pocket watch back in his waistcoat pocket, and threw his arms in the air. "Thirty miles an hour, and nothing's beaten it – a clear winner our Robert's 'Rocket'."

Programmes went up in the air. People cheered and waved. And then Mr Robert Stephenson himself was climbing down from the engine. He was striding towards them smiling. And suddenly Robert Stephenson was reaching out his hand to Jack.

"The boy who saved my topper! It's good to see you again, lad. I think you two lads deserve a ride on 'Rocket' up here with me and my father. What do you say?" Jack opened his mouth to speak but no words came.

"Oh yes please, Sir," said Tom. "Please."

The smell of the smoke. The heat from the burning coals. The steam screeching out. It was like nothing Jack could have imagined. With the wind beating his cheeks and the countryside flashing by, he felt he was zooming to the edge of the world on the winning engine. Up above him 'Rocket's' white smoke curled out like a quilt. It was all too marvellous to believe. Jack shut his eyes. Now he was on top of the world, flying along beside the two great men who'd made this wonderful iron horse. And Robert himself was standing with his chin tilted proudly upwards, enjoying every second too.

"This is only the beginning of things, Jack," said Robert. "Next year this line from Liverpool to Manchester will open. Others too. Soon there will be railway lines all over the country and iron horses everywhere."

Jack took a deep breath and let it out slowly. He couldn't wait for it all to happen. He thought of his own father and smiled to himself. Would the grain prices be better still in Manchester? If so their wheat would certainly be going there next year – and with his father's blessing.